I want this

FOR *US*

RUMI TSUCHIHASHI

I WANT THIS FOR US

THE TINY MOMENTS THAT GIVE MARRIAGE A CHANCE

TINY WONDERS PRESS

SEATTLE, WA

Copyright © 2024 by Rumi Tsuchihashi

All rights reserved. No part of this publication may be reproduced, distributed, or transmitted in any form or by any means, including photocopying, recording, or other electronic or mechanical methods, without the prior written permission of the publisher, except in the case of brief quotations embodied in critical reviews and certain other noncommercial uses permitted by copyright law. For permission requests, write to the publisher at the email address below.

Tiny Wonders Press
hello@rumitsuchihashi.com

I Want This For Us / Rumi Tsuchihashi
—1st ed. ISBN 979-8-9897167-1-5

Contents.

For Ojii-chan

We talk so much of light,
please
let me speak on behalf

of the good dark. Let us
talk more of how dark

the beginning of a day is.

-How Dark The Beginning

Maggie Smith

There's beauty in the darkness.

What do you want to remember from your life, most of all?

For me, it's the little things. A morsel of something unusually delicious. A song overheard. Something beautiful falling from the sky. These moments are especially stirring if they happen when I'm feeling lost and frightened.

We all go through dark places we call, "times like this."

Maybe you're smack in the middle of a "times like this."

If so, you'll be comforted by this book.

I Want This For Us is a radical celebration of the murky, poignant space between the end of a first marriage and the beginning of a second one.

Maybe you've noticed, but "divorced" is a forced identity; not-yet-remarried people must check that box on every official form, even if their marriage was dissolved eons ago.

We're conditioned to think of such transitional spaces as "lag time" — neither here nor there, or even nothingness.

And yet, as my friend Simone says, "There's so much happening in the lag time. There's no lag in lag time."

She's right: if we aren't careful, we'll fixate on the hopefully more secure

future and miss the gorgeous life
happening in the liminal space.

And what we want to remember from
our life most of all will pass us by.

I wrote this book to appreciate all the
moments, bitter and sweet, that fed
into my happy second marriage. I
wrote to not forget what morsels I
unearthed, and to offer you a taste.

I hope you'll be comforted, inspired,
and excited to find deliciousness in
your own "times like this."

Let's go see what we can unearth
together in the Good Dark.

Dawn Till Dusk

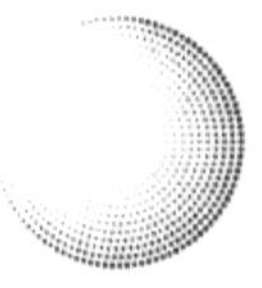

Gone rogue.

The tapas on the table—grilled meats, roasted potatoes, and marinated vegetables—were down to just a single bite on each of the tiny plates. It had to be said now, "it," which had been on my mind for several months.

"If circumstances were different, I'd want more," I blurted out.

"I love our friendship, and, but, I'd want more, different . . ." I added, without finishing the sentence.

What my lips withheld, my hands took upon themselves to say, clearing a

path between the little white dishes,
taking hold of the long fingers resting
on the edge of the other side of the
table, squeezing them tightly.

Would you like some help with making better choices?

I lived through two long winters of separation in my forties; one from my first husband before the marriage officially ended, and one after that tapas date when Pete vanished from my life.

During the first winter, I obsessively read every article for women who fall for unavailable men.

I read them on my side of the cold bed so I could figure out my part in the divorce, and make sure I'd never, ever, ever feel this searing pain again.

I read them in a parked car after a miserable blind date with a Mr. Available; so happy to be alone again, but also tense with worry I'd stay alone for eternity.

And I read them as I stood in the mile long, Sunday afternoon grocery checkout line.

"Your illness is curable," each article suggested, helpfully. "And we'll help you make better choices."

I felt comforted enough to eventually stop reading these things.

Then, a second winter of separation arrived, and I was right back at it.

I wanted to stop attracting unavailable men once and for all. Forgetting them seemed like the right choice. The healthy choice.

But this time, some part of me knew the compulsive reading was smoke in mirrors.

Secretly, I wanted to go on being a messy woman, someone who gets that not every person who crosses your path is available in the ways she wants them to be—and chooses to love them imperfectly anyway.

The condition I have might be an illness.

Or maybe it's a sign of womanly holiness.

First impression.

Let me tell you about the first time I met Pete.

It happened on a dry but bone-chilling December afternoon, at the Japanese Garden in Seattle, Washington where we both worked.

He was the new head gardener, and I, the Program Manager of two years, came outside my office to say hi.

"Welcome! I'm Rumi," I said.

Pete acknowledged me from twelve feet away with a nod.

I meant to tell him a bit about what I do, but he stayed so quiet—and unmoving—I didn't know where to begin.

"Well, you know where to find me," he said, finally, grandly gesturing to the garden beyond him.

And that was that.

I wasn't sure he even heard my name. Or cared whether he had or not.

"And you know where to find me," I said, possibly aloud, which would've meant I was talking to myself since Pete was long gone and not paying me any attention.

As first impressions go, this one could have been better.

FOUR

Worth a second try.

"So, why Japanese gardens?" I asked Pete.

It had been a month since the first hello, which was so off putting, I'd basically avoided him.

Still, I couldn't shake my curiosity. How did this long-limbed white man from El Paso, Texas with cool retro glasses and an armful of tattoos turn into *the* local expert at tending to Japanese-style gardens?

His profession is a serious niche within a niche.

There's no real training for this specialty, and barely a name for it.

His answer came swiftly. "Narrative," he said.

I grimaced in confusion. *Narrative?*

"Narrative," Pete repeated as if I didn't hear him the first time.

Here we are at another dead end, I thought. I can't talk to this guy.

But then, my heart took over my mouth.

"Tell me more," I said softly. And here's what I learned:

In a garden, all its elements—plants, water, rocks, structures, earth, sky, creatures, and people—relate to each other, beautifully but unpredictably.

And the gardener gets to shape and tell the story of how nature meets nurture.

***

Ahh. Well.

As second impressions go, this one couldn't have been more magical.

FIVE

Block Letters.

I fell in love with the handwriting before I even had an inkling I'd fall in love with the man.

The letters were in all caps, and so tiny you'd think this person learned to write on five-millimeter graph paper.

This handwriting had personality.

Delicately strong. Quietly imposing. Gently intimidating.

Simultaneously aware of rules and busting expectations.

It suggested that the writer was someone who holds opposites as if they were magnets; properly positioned to attract, not repel.

The lettering made me swoon.

So, before I really knew the man, I started sneaking out of the office with the handwritten notes he'd tossed in the bin.

SIX

Try, try again.

The first time I tasted injera, the garden was blanketed in a foot of snow.

It was crazy of me to drive the treacherous roads just for winter wonderland photos, but I didn't try the last time I had the chance, and I regretted it.

When I completed the photo shoot and headed to the break room to warm up, I was surprised to see the lights on.

I gingerly opened the steel door and out came another surprise: the scent of stewed meats and warm spices, and

the sight of Pete warming up
Ethiopian food.

Soon, his lunch became my lunch.

***

I tore a piece of injera—a flat,
pockmarked bread—with my icy
fingers and brought it to my lips. The
first bite was a shock of sourness.

Pete was too busy scooping up a piece
of glossy, cognac-colored piece of
chicken onto his plate to notice the
look on my face.

"I didn't get the job the first time
around," he said out of nowhere.

This was news to me. "Wow. Applying
again must have been nerve wracking.
You had to deal with the rejection once
already," I said.

His eyes looked off into the distance. Maybe he was just savoring his chicken, but he looked like he was daydreaming, wondering where he'd be today if he hadn't risked failure and tried to get the job one more time.

Where would he be? And what kind of sad, cold lunch would I be eating alone right now?

But here we were together. Because we both found the courage to face regret or disappointment and try again.

It stuns me to think how close I came to this delightfully warm, spicy lunch on a cold, snowy day not happening.

And for you not to be here, reading about it.

Oh, and for the record, the injera tasted like sunshine from the second bite on.

SEVEN

Ancient love language.

At the end of one hard day, I hugged him inside my office. He was stiff at first, then, suddenly and inexplicably, his torso went limp, softening into mine. I heard the tiniest of squeaks come from inside his chest, a cry of relief, perhaps, or a language of heart connection that predates all human language.

EIGHT

What would you do for a shred of praise?

Here I am, absentmindedly washing my hands in the break room. As I shut the faucet off, I hear someone say, "I'd walk for miles barefoot across shards of glass for it." *Ouch!*

The towel dispenser squeaks when I turn it, and then, the economy-grade brown pulp scrapes against my palm, making it near impossible to hear the next few words.

But soon, I piece things together: Pete was talking about praise. How he craves it.

This guy looks so confident to me. He takes pruners to the branches of prized specimens and clips with zero hesitation. And his movements are so precise, it's like watching his hands do a ballet dance.

And yet.

How is praise so seductive that he'd walk for miles barefoot across shards of glass—leaving a gruesome trail of blood, no doubt—to get it?

I wince. And wonder:

Has he heard the Mary Oliver poem, Wild Geese?

The one about repenting, despair, and letting our soft animal bodies love what they love?

I make a note to ask Pete someday.

NINE

Snip.

The Shinto spring blessing of the Japanese Garden is scheduled to start in seventeen minutes. That's when I realize I haven't gathered the ceremonial camellia bouquet the reverend asked me to prepare.

I run around looking for Pete, the head gardener. I poke him from behind as he comes out of the shed.

After he turns around startled, I breathlessly say, "I . . . cut flowers . . . need now." So much adrenaline is coursing through me that I've forgotten how to speak English.

With a softened look, he hands me a
pair of shears. They're ink black
except for the gleaming, newly-
sharpened silver blades.

I've never physically altered any part
of this meticulously maintained
garden before. I stare at the blades,
then at Pete, and the blades again,
both my hands and eyes trembling.

"I trust you," he says.

The word trust sends electricity
through my veins.

He trusts me. With pruners. With
making permanent cuts.

He trusts me more than I trust myself
right now—and that makes me giddy!

Like a child getting away with
something, I walk-run to the nearest

camellia bush with shears in hand,
excited to hear the first crisp snip.

TEN

Nowhere to hide.

I smugly carried a heaving boxload of event supplies from my tiny office to my car.

I was so proud of myself for packing everything I needed to work from home the next day into one box—and saving myself an extra trip.

But when I got to the car, I realized I'd left my purse behind.

Even though I felt stupid inside, I decided to conceal it and walk chin up back to the office, as if taking two trips had been my plan all along. On my way back to the office, I passed Pete, who was pruning the pine tree in the courtyard.

"What'd you forget?" he asked.

"How did you know I forgot something?" I snapped back. It was too loud and sharp, an unfit response to the gently posed question. My act of bravado was exposed, and the mounting embarrassment made me prickly, porcupine-like.

"I saw you do what people do when they forget things," he said, miming the body language I used while standing by the car. Then, he noticed the look on my face and abruptly quit.

Here, I thought I was good at pretending.

It turned out I hadn't had a place to hide. Not from him, anyway.

ELEVEN

Piano Sonata No. 11.

I don't yet know this in 2016, but between Pete's absence—and a global pandemic–I'll come to know silence like never before.

And years after, that silence will break and open to a joyful cacophony of voices coming from the kitchen.

From my office a floor above, I'll hear Reina's melodic high notes, Pete's percussive keys in the lower octave, and Kai's loud chords.

This sound—so reminiscent of Mozart's Piano Sonata No. 11—will melt me from the inside out.

TWELVE

Pressure valve release.

One Monday morning at work, I run into Rae at a fork in the gravel path.

"What do you do to let off steam?" Rae says after a quick catch-up.

Her brows are furrowed, and her mouth is slightly contorted. I take it she's concerned about the child support battle and the toll it's taking on me.

Just then, Pete approaches. He's quiet as a mouse, but his eyes are sparkling with curiosity, ears wide open to hear my answer.

"Oh," I say brightly. "I go to Dance
Church!"

Here's the gist of what I share:

On Sundays at 10 a.m., bodies of all
shapes and sizes unite in a club-like
setting.

Major Lazer remixes of Justin Bieber
tunes and old-school Ke$ha boom out
of a pair of eight-foot speakers, and a
hundred of us groove to the music.

All the mirrors are covered up on
purpose, so we focus on being in the
moment, not on how we look.

 "And just when you think you're
having the best time, Kate, the teacher
yells at us, 'Get lower!' And
we do a third round of deep squats," I
say. "These pulses are so painful it
makes me want to cry."

As soon as I say this, I avert my eyes
from Rae and Pete's riveted gaze
because I feel the tears coming, just
like I do at Dance Church.

It's like my sorrow is stored in my
inner thighs, and the "Get lower!"
command releases the pressure valve.

And I cry a river of sweat and tears.

What pours out of me is always so
scorching hot, it steams.

THIRTEEN

Unreal.

Libbie walks me to the bench shaded by the three tall ginkgo trees. We sit side by side, noticing the bright afternoon sun casting dark, dancing leaf-shaped shadows on the gravel paths.

This is my first visit back to the Japanese Garden since I left my job there, and four months after the tapas outing with Pete.

"You know, dear," she says, then stops. The pause gives me a moment to note how the word "dear" is said with a thicker than usual Tasmanian accent. It sounded like *DEE-ya, and it echoed.*

DEE-ya
DEE-ya
DEE-ya.

It turns out, she wanted to tell me about a dream.

In this dream, Pete—who's in a committed relationship—had confessed to her that something vivid, saucy, and illicit had happened between him and me.

"I don't know if I want you to tell me there is or isn't a basis for this dream in real life," Libbie says with a shiver.

Nothing is going on between us, we aren't even talking, I tell Libbie. But she isn't comforted by this news.

"What I saw was so real," she says with a sigh, "No offense, but it was more real than you sitting next to me right now."

Me, too, I think. Living in what feels like a perpetual transition, a liminal space, sometimes the veil between dreams and reality get so thin, I don't know what's real from what isn't, or where or who I am.

"Mmm," I say, and rest my palm on the back of her delicate, age-spotted hand, cool to the touch even on this unseasonably warm day.

I wait for heat to transfer from my body to hers.

I wait to feel something real.

FOURTEEN

Not yours.

In the spring of 2017, I was proofreading a manuscript at my new job when I felt a switch flip.

On that page was a line drawing of a strong hand. The caption said hands tell stories about the places they've been, the things they've created, the beings they've caressed and cradled.

I was besieged with the urge to bust out of the office clutching that manuscript, rush to the Japanese Garden, and say, "See this, Pete? This is about you! It's your narrative."

But that wasn't an option, even if I were crazy enough to act on the impulse.

Pete and I weren't speaking then. Our connection had gone cold six months earlier, days after the tapas date, when I made our platonic friendship awkward by reaching across the table.

I wanted to hold those hands.

Instead, I clutched those stapled pages, briefly pressing them against my aching chest.

Is it just me, or do some painful moments scream, "Remember this!" to you as it's unfolding?

When I was ready to let go of the stapled pages, I pulled out my phone.

I broke the rules and snuck a picture of that not-yet-published book.

FIFTEEN

Oh, F.

He meets me in Washington Park. I've been side-eyeing a couple; they've almost vacated a bench for the last ten minutes; my falafels, meanwhile, have gone cold.

"I got tickets," F says with a smile. I notice he doesn't say *the* tickets to the hottest Broadway show of 1999, the one we'd agreed to see. My smile freezes in place.

He's sits down where the couple had been and reaches up for the brown paper bag I'm holding. *Wait, was the sight of a tall white man the signal they needed to leave?*

"Oh, a scalper offered me two tickets to see Billy Joel at Madison Square Garden. I thought about that but turned him down," F adds casually as he unwraps the foil of his sandwich.

I do a mental inventory.

Hadn't I told him how hard I fought to connect with Mom growing up?

Hadn't I told him how meaningful our mutual love of The Stranger *album was to me?*

And what I'd give to see Billy Joel live at Madison Square Garden someday?

I told him, didn't I?

***

I will eventually marry F.

I will scratch my head, again and again
for years on end, and ask myself, "I
told him, didn't I?" until I wonder if
I'm losing my mind.

I will forget most of the incidents,
because they'll bleed into one big
sorrow bucket of a story.

But I will remember this day.

I will remember this day because my
early love of *The Stranger* was so
meaningful.

And *The Stranger* still has gifts for me,
beautiful surprises yet to be revealed,
if I could just hold on, hold on.

SIXTEEN

Read the memo, darling.

From age three on, Reina made me cheerful notes with gusto. They became so bountiful many went unnoticed or forgotten.

But one that she slipped under my closed bedroom door truly stood out.

"I heard you crying and I want you to know there's no reason for you to say you want to die," the note said.

Ugh. I wish she hadn't heard me say that. The words came squirting out sideways one night because hard things had piled up.

1. I got fired from my new job.
2. I was about to lose the house.
3. I didn't know if I'd ever see Pete again.
4. I was a full-time single mom.

"If you feel that way," Reina went on to say, "look at the cons instead of the pros and you will feel better."

Look at the cons instead of the pros.

Ha, I snorted. She probably didn't mean that! But still, so sweet.

I taped the note to the door to remember Reina's kindness. Then, rereading it for the 100th time, I wondered, *did* she mean it?

Because facing the sorrow is unthinkably terrifying—until you do. Then, the denial fades, and it feels so. Much. Better. Just like Reina said.

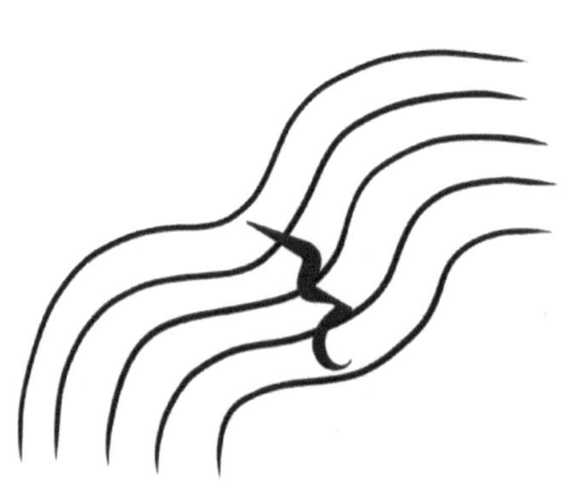

SEVENTEEN

End of the road.

A hundred of us at Dance Church are in corpse pose, with Boyz II Men crooning in surround sound overhead.

Pain in my head, oh I'd rather be dead...

Spinnin' around and around...

That's right, it's almost Valentine's Day. I've denied this holiday even exists for so long.

Still I can't let go...

Buddy, is it time for you and me to let go anyway? And surrender to the fact that we have no control over whether we'll ever find lasting romantic love?

I've come to the end of the road . . . it's unnatural. . . you belong to me . . .

Oof.

Yes, baby my heart is lonely. . .

My heart hurts baby. . . I feel pain too. . .

Ohmygod, stop it! Do we have be like this? I'm going to die of agony.

Baby please. . .

No! I roll my eyes inside their sockets.

Still I can't let go. . .

I can't take it anymore. I'm past cringing. Shame has engulfed me, and I want the earth to swallow me whole.

And, then, ta-da! My insides come
alive again with a new thought:

How lucky are you?! You found
someone you care about this much.
Lucky, lucky, lucky you!

We've come to the end of the road...

Still I can't let go...

So you hurt, but what else are we here
on earth to do but give love away?

And with that, I decide I will not deny
this Valentine's Day. I will celebrate
how lucky I am to have found Pete, to
be as fond of his as I am, to adore and
admire him from a distance if I never
see him again.

*Although we've come to the end of the
road.*

You belong to me... I belong to you!

EIGHTEEN

The kiss of death.

And just like that, the wait was over. An email from Pete arrived on February 14, 2018.

Eleven months after the tapas dinner where I'd said too much and made our friendship untenable, here we were together again, having drinks at a 1920s-themed hotel bar at the bottom of Queen Anne Avenue.

I learned he was no longer romantically attached.

And that he'd need a ride home.

"While we're at it," I said with a huff as we climbed uphill to my car, "would you like to walk an extra block and check out the view from Kerry Viewpoint?"

He agreed, and I reached for his hand. We walked in silence.

And there it was, the view: Downtown Seattle and the Space Needle awash in twinkling lights, shimmery and hopeful, Elliot Bay reflecting it back.

I gasped in delight. But before I could fully take in the beauty, I felt large hands on either side of my shoulders.

Then, my lips were no longer exposed to the freezing wind.

It was the end of what was and the beginning of what we don't yet know. Here we were in the dark, having the kiss of death and rebirth.

Dusk Till Dawn

NINETEEN

Try, try again, one more time.

Before we were a couple, Pete had heard enough drivel about my divorce in the break room at work. Now that we were together, I wanted to be judicious with stories about my past.

But when I saw *The Stranger* at the bottom of his bookshelf where he kept all his vinyl, I:

1. Pulled it out, and sniffed it before holding it to my chest, just as I'd done as an eight-year-old with my mother's

version of the same Billy Joel
record,
2. Told Pete how much I loved
the moment the needle
dropped and you heard the
little scratch
3. Asked if we could play it,
starting with the B-side.

And then, I told him about that day in
Washington Park.

"Biggest mistake he ever made," I
said, referring to my ex-husband.

I will never again silence my
disappointments, I thought to myself,
self-love blooming large in my chest.

Because we all want to transcend our
mistakes and be the best version of
ourselves with and for our next loves.

But will I? Only time will tell.

TWENTY

Ground zero.

His new mattress hadn't arrived, so, we spent our first night together lying on top of a pile of blankets on the cold hard floor of his living room.

Soon, his mattress came, but we'd end up back on the floor sometimes.

"If I have you, blankets, and a solid floor beneath me, I'll be okay, no matter what," I'd say.

Now, the floor doesn't seem so inviting. But I try not to forget what I said. I try not to forget how more than okay ground zero is.

TWENTY-ONE

Tiny, potent love.

"What would you like me to make?" Pete asked over the phone. He was inviting me over for dinner for the first time.

"Beef bourguignon!" I said.

I marveled at the decisiveness of my request for a dish I hadn't eaten or even thought of in years.

The night arrived.

As I descended the stairs to his front door, I could smell the red wine

reduction seeping into softened
carrots and pearl onions. An invisible
steam was rising and swirling into the
bone-chilling damp air.

I watched Pete wipe his hands on his
apron on the other side of the glass
door. He let me in. After a quick kiss,
he excused himself to return to the
stove.

I gingerly approached the partially set
dining table alone with the
naughtiness of a child who tip-toes up
to the Christmas tree, trying guess
what gifts are hidden in each box. I
don't know what I thought I could get
a sneak peek at, but my heart skipped
at the anticipation.

And then, I saw them.

Three shallow, blue-rimmed bowls,
each the diameter of a large coin.

In one, finely chopped curly parsley.

In another, freshly ground black
pepper.

And in the last, flaky sea salt,
sparkling all diamond-like at the
edges under the dim light.

I had to contain a squeal.

I love tiny things that speak volumes
about care, precision, and delight.

Sometimes our subconscious minds
sense what's possible and do things
that don't make sense.

Asking for a stew I rarely eat gave Pete
a reason to put out those tiny vessels
of love—and for me to sprinkle my
first home cooked meal with him with
magical fairy dust.

TWENTY-TWO

The special spot.

I sat there at 2:45 am one night, raging at a missing someone who eventually stayed gone for good.

Then, Kai noticed I'd taken to sitting there in the corner of the kitchen, my butt on the cold tile floor on purpose.

So, there I was when years later, my future husband called to say, "I think I'm falling in love with you."

I had to sell that house. Along with the special spot. But sometimes, I catch my body searching for it, craving and aching for one last sit.

TWENTY-THREE

Well meaning.

The day he brought over the surprise gift, Pete's blue gray eyes were extra sparkly behind his partly rimless glasses.

"For you!" he said, and handed me a bottle of Wegman's Stainless Steel Cleaner for my dirty, greasy stove.

I smiled and cupped the small metal container in my palms like a bottle of perfume. "Ooooo," I said, expecting words of appreciation would come.

But all that came was the hot shame of him witnessing my poor household hygiene—and a waft of armpit stink.

TWENTY-FOUR

Beholding beauty.

We stayed at the museum for three and a half hours and didn't see the permanent exhibits. Well, almost.

"I just have to see the one," Pete said.

And we landed in front of the Rothko.

One soft block of color stacks atop another, with tiny gaps in between; sienna, pink, muted red orange. It's one of those "My toddler could do that" modern abstract paintings.

I watch as the edges of his eyes soften,
then moisten.

They say beauty is in the eye of the
beholder.

And I am witness to the beholder of
beauty I do not readily see—but feel as
a crackling, thunderous energy.

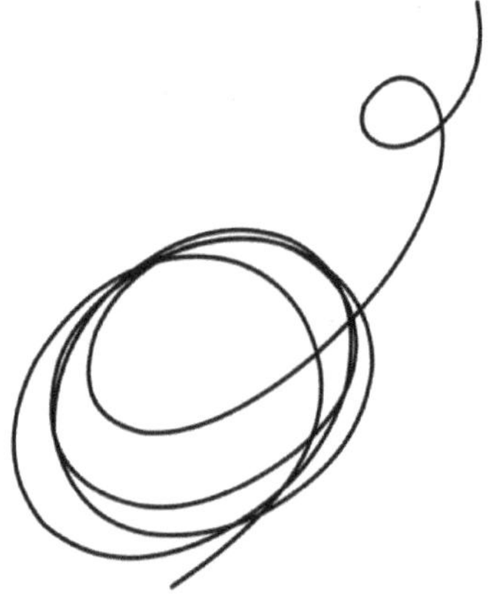

TWENTY-FIVE

A lover's calculation.

The first time I brought food to Pete's apartment, I also brought my curling zester. It wasn't anything fancy—a tool I picked up at IKEA for a dollar or two— but it did a marvelous job of pulling long, fine ribbons off a fresh lemon. I was fond of it.

"Do you have one of these?" I asked.

He had many tools I did not: a cherry pit remover, an oyster shucker, and a microplane. He shook his head no.

"I'll leave this here with you!" I said enthusiastically, without thinking. "I've got another one," I added.

It was a lie. I did not own another IKEA curling zester.

Did I mention I loved this tool? I did. I used it often to add a little flourish to salads, ice cream, you name it.

At least once a week, I'd think of pulling it out and remember it wasn't in my drawer anymore.

Over the years, I had a million opportunities to come clean and bring the zester back home.

Instead, when tension rose between us and I feared our relationship might not last, I'd think about the stupid curling zester and seethe.

Lovers calculate the risks and rewards of the strangest things.

TWENTY-SIX

Palmed.

Pete's hands are so big, they can swallow mine whole, making them feel like they're swaddled in a slightly scratchy but warm wool blanket.

Sometimes, the feeling takes me back to a moment I shared with *ojii-chan*, my grandfather, when I was four; a memory so precious I wrote a little essay about it.

When 'Where Our Palms Touch,' was published in the *New York Times*, I excitedly texted my parents with the good news.

Three days later, I hear from my dad:

"Please tell me what 'a liquid tingle' springing from our palms means," he asked.

He must have spent all those days Googling the shit out of my carefully crafted expression of simple, intimate love—and come up empty handed.

I felt a kind of sad affection for Dad.

I wished I could just squeeze the answer through the phone so he could stop analyzing. And just feel it.

TWENTY-SEVEN

Wild Geese.

“Have you heard the poem *Wild Geese?*”

We're headed south on I-5 through Longview, Washington. The windshield wipers are squeaking away working double time; in my driving experience, the sky here is always crying buckets of tears.

“I don't think so,” Pete says, eyes on the wet road.

“The opening lines are, 'You do not have to be good. / You do not have to walk on your knees / for a hundred

miles through the desert repenting.'
And it makes me think of you."

I sense him sinking deeper into the
passenger seat, like he's dropped the
tension he's used to holding, and
letting himself be held.

I ask if that resonates, and he nods.
In eighteen hours, I'll spot and snap
up the thick white hardcover edition of
Devotions, a compilation of Ms.
Oliver's most celebrated poems, at my
beloved Powells Books.

In 36 hours, I'll put a bookmark in the
page where *Wild Geese* is. I'll leave it
conspicuously behind at Pete's
apartment.

And a week later, I'll be astonished to
find the fruits of Pete's new daily
practice on his kitchen table; seven
sheets of paper, each one filled with
every word of *Wild Geese*, in that tiny
block letter handwriting I so love.

TWENTY-EIGHT

Pruning.

As someone who sculpts trees into works of fine art, Pete has taught hundreds of pruning workshops.

People always ask him how he knows what branches to cut out.

"The question isn't, 'What do I take out?'" he answers every time, "It's 'What am I keeping?'"

On trees and in life, you want your attention on what you want to grow and expand—and release everything but that.

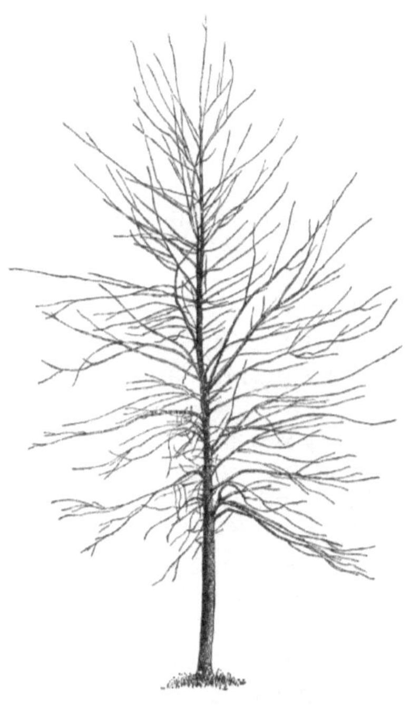

TWENTY-NINE

Everything is going to be okay.

This is what Pete most wants to hear when he's upset.

"I don't want you to swoop in and save the day when things go awry," he tells me one day.

We'd just survived an emotional storm—what was it over, a jar of peanut butter and a half-finished can of soda on the counter, left there as if the offending child just assumed Pete would clean it up for them?

"I don't want you snatching things from me; I just want to hear you say the words I want to hear," he adds.

"But that would be a lie," I reply, "I can't know if everything's going to be okay."

He gives me a look as painfully contorted as the humanoid in Edvard Munch's famous painting, *The Scream*.

Fast forward five years.

Pete, me, the naughty cat, and the two teens who sometimes lack self-awareness are living under one roof.

I hear Pete's loud sigh echoing through the house as he's tying up the bag of kitchen trash.

"May I?" I ask, and he hands it over silently.

My heart is pounding as I descend the stairs and head outside. I am dreading being called out yet again for reflexively swooping in to "fix."

The prickle of agitation is getting
intense, and poking my face, throat,
arms, and legs from the inside out.

I just want to make things better, I
think. *Can't I do that?*

When I drop of the trash bag into the
bin with a thud, I hear an answer.

I take a deep breath and rehearse what
I'll say when I reach the top of the
stairs and return to the kitchen.

"Sweetheart," I say to Pete.

I wrap my arms around his waist,
making a hug he can't return because
he's got a wet rag in his hand.

"It's okay, everything's going to be
okay," I say with my face turned
sideways, my cheek pressing the
words I want to believe—and he longs
to hear—onto his chest like a tattoo
on the heart.

THIRTY

Nothing ventured, nothing gained, Part 1.

After pacing the halls of the open office on the 19th floor at my newest job, looking for a private space, I give up and stand near the elevators to finish the phone call.

My friend asks, "So, how are things with Pete?"

"Good," I say, "They're going good."

There's a pause. I sense friction in the silence.

"I respect that you're trying to do things differently from your marriage to F, but I feel like I'm in the dark about how your relationship works," the friend says.

I grind my teeth, side to side, hearing this.

It would've been easy to blame the setting, to offer to call back later and continue this conversation when I'm in a better space.

Even easier still to say, "I'm sorry," and, like old times, bond by sharing the less than savory aspects of my partner, things he does that hurts my feelings or pisses me off.

But here's what I say instead.

"You're right; I am doing things differently. If there's a problem between us, if something's bothering me, I make sure he's the first to know. And—" I take a breath.

"When I do, there's not much to say about the situation anymore."

I don't recall how the conversation ended. But I remember how my face reddened, and my phone got slick with sweat in my right hand.

Was I insensitive to my friend's unspoken feelings?

Should I have waited before I spoke after all?

What damage might I have inflicted on our friendship just now?

I don't have an answer to those questions, just a conviction.

If there's a problem between us or something is bothering me, Pete will be the first to know.

THIRTY-ONE

Nothing ventured, nothing gained, Part 2.

On March 24, 2020, the State of Washington enacts the first Covid-19 lockdown mandate.

There will be no school for children.

No office work, and no leaving the house for anything besides bare necessities.

No seeing anyone outside of your household.

I want Pete to move in.

Or else, for him to decide we're one
household with a "satellite location,"
his apartment.

I hear no and no.

I feel like the skies above Longview,
Washington, and let fat drops of water
rain down my cheeks.

"There's not much to say about the
situation anymore," I remember
saying to my friend about addressing
disagreements between Pete and me
head on, not even two months earlier.

Now, I wish I could go on complaining.

Now I wish my words hadn't been so
spot on.

THIRTY-TWO

Nothing ventured, nothing gained, part 3.

Four years and a month after the first Covid-19 lockdown, I'll be adding a watercolor flourish to our wedding invitations at the kitchen table Pete and I share.

I will get frustrated with my work.

I will ask Pete, who's a better visual artist than I am, to give things a shot.

And as I watch him play with the ink and brush, I'll remember that watercolor, like a relationship, works best if you trust it, and let the hue move around and rest where it wants.

Revenge pink.

My ex-husband hated the way I taped up paint chips all over the house, and studied the way they changed colors with the time of day, the weather, and the seasons.

The one consolation about moving homes against my will was that I'd get to pick whatever bedroom wall color I wanted—and be as stickler about the decision-making process as I pleased.

So, of course, I selected a blush pink from Benjamin Moore in a snap.

I wanted this soft, enveloping, sensual
hue to greet me gently when I awoke.
And cocoon me each night as I fell
asleep.

I told Pete this wall color backstory the
morning after the first night he slept
over at my house.

"It's all those things and sexy, too,"
he said of Revenge Pink, and taught
me to enjoy studying the shadows cast
on it by the half-closed curtains.

Soft, enveloping, sensual—and sexy. I
suddenly realized Revenge Pink was a
long-dormant quality of me.

I was projecting onto my walls the
person I forgot I was and wanted
desperately to reclaim. Revenge pink
nourished my hope for love—
romantic love and self-love—after a
shattering divorce.

*****

For three years after, I studied how
Revenge Pink changes with the time
day, the weather, and the seasons.

I studied the shadows half-closed
curtains cast onto the blank walls.

I made Revenge Pink—soft,
enveloping, sensual—and sexy! —my
measurable, my mark of well-being
and guiding light.

However.

Life had its own agenda, including:

- My ex-husband getting lymphoma and very nearly dying from it

- An angry Reina insisting I not invite Pete over so often (understandably, but still)

- Keeping Kai and Reina at home with me full-time for seventeen months—thanks Covid lockdowns!

- Starting a full-time job just weeks before that lock down, and finding out me and my boss were a very bad match

- Holding down a copywriting side hustle through this all so I could accomplish my goal of buying a new home

- Home prices jumping 25% year-over-year and inciting insane bidding wars all over the city

I didn't feel soft, enveloping, sensual—and sexy all that much.

I wasn't sure I ever would.

And yet.

Breathing those vibes in morning and night, I was making progress in my reclamation, bit by bit, without even realizing it.

And one day, my inside reality and outside reality came together.

There I was, packing up the Revenge Pink bedroom to move to a house I bought and would share with someone who loved me deeply, permanently taped up paint chips and all.

THIRTY-FOUR

When one door closes.

The house I was leaving sat on a well-trafficked intersection. It was the perfect spot to gift used household items—passersby would snap them up within hours.

It was time to let go of a few dinged-up chairs and tables. I'd hauled them from Seattle to New York City and back again. I loved the stories they told—the good parts of life I'd lived before I met Pete.

So, as I carried them one last time, tears fell.

Minutes later, my cheeks still wet, I
peeked out of the living room window
and saw excited faces. The new owners
of the furniture were beaming as they
opened the trunk to fit their new
treasures in.

My story with these tiny furnishings
had ended—and theirs was just
beginning.

THIRTY-FIVE

Another door opens to—tacos.
So many tacos.

Maybe he knew already because he's from Texas, or maybe it became clear when we moved in together, but tacos are Pete's #1 love language.

He'd won over all of my friends and my kids' friends with his succulent meats, colorful arrays of sides, and perfectly charred corn and flour tortillas even before we lived together.

But then, once we had him living under the same roof, one of Reina's friends was over for dinner every Tuesday night.

More kept coming, until a dozen of them showed up for Reina's birthday tacos. Two years in a row.

The menu came to include birria tacos. And Impossible meat with roasted potatoes tacos for the vegetarians. And fire roasted, pureed green chili salsa served alongside the classic Pico de Gallo.

Pete even overcame is aversion to buying and serving avocados—on the account that they make a mockery of you, being bad when they look good, more than half the time.

And he travelled to Japan with two pounds of quesadilla cheese and his proprietary seasonings in tow, and regaled my parents, siblings, and nieces and nephews with a Taco Tuesday in Tokyo event that will go down in history as one of the tastiest family meals we've ever shared.

Wherever Pete is, if there is sorrow, there will be tacos.

Wherever he is, if there is joy, there will also be tacos.

***

Sometimes in relationships, we enter murky waters where we must ask deep, hard questions. At others, the next right move is gloriously clear, and we must nourish ourselves to walk that path.

Either way, Pete, bless his heart, will be there with his strong, muscular Popeye forearms loaded with tacos. Tacos. And more tacos.

THIRTY-SIX

His beginnings.

Once, his mother told me one of Pete's baby stories.

Seeing as he was the youngest of three, the children all close in age, she had her hands full then. To her delight and astonishment, Pete could keep quiet and entertain himself alone in the crib for many hours.

The mother in me heard the brag in her voice.

The mother in me also detected an unspoken request for validation.

Nothing was wrong with this scene, right?

"I mean, I came and went, and he looked just the same," she added, circling back to the original conversation after a long tangent. I nodded, though I wasn't sure what I was agreeing to.

Meanwhile, my heart had already left the room, searching for Pete, wanting to hold him.

THIRTY-SEVEN

My beginnings.

Going through my baby pictures, I thought of something my mother once told me—a story about a walk we took with *Koiwa-no-obaachan*, her mother-in-law, my paternal grandmother.

As a poorly coordinated toddler, I regularly scraped the heels of my hands and my knees and cried about it. And sure enough, that day, I also tripped and fell.

"You're okay," Mom said.

It took a few minutes, but eventually, I got up and dusted my knees. Then,

and only then, did my mother
approach me.

"Your *obaachan* was furious. 'What
kind of mother lets her child cry alone
like that?'" said Mom, mimicking my
grandmother's puffed-up face. Her
cheeks reddened.

Then, Mom was there but not there
anymore. I remember her faraway
eyes and the way she smelled like
talcum powder.

I felt my spine straighten and
shoulders slump, a strange mixture of
pride and pitifulness.

Recalling this conversation decades
later, the mother in me heard the brag
in my mother's voice.

The mother in me also detected an
unspoken request for validation.

"I mean, why coddle a child so she
can't even recover from her falls?" I
remember Mom saying, her eyes
suddenly looking straight into mine.

I looked at my faded pictures,
searching the eyes of my younger self
for an answer.

I wondered if, more than praise for her
strength, determination, and self–
sufficiency, she'd like a pair of warm
arms to hold her.

If you're coupled with someone who has experienced even a teensy bit of early childhood neglect, and now carries the weight of the world on their shoulders, you should broach this question with maximum caution (or better yet, avoid it altogether.)

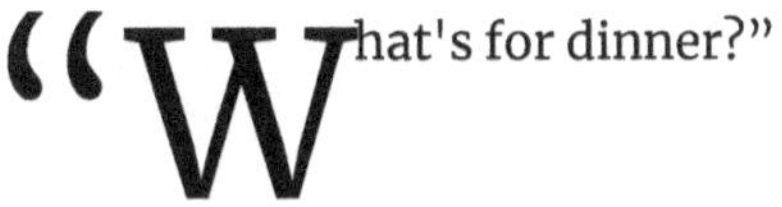

Tension.

"He's gone," I say to Reina without turning to her. I'm in the middle of composing a sentence on the screen, annoyed by the disruption.

"He's GONE? What do you mean?" Her voice is louder this time, alarmed.

Feeling guilty for startling her like this, I stop typing.

"For the weekend. Pete's doing a whole weekend job. Gone for the weekend," I say, taking my hands off

the keyboard and placing them in my
lap as I meet Reina's bugged-out eyes.

I watch her torso slump in relief.

"You made me think he was gone-
gone, like out of our lives," she says as
she continues down the hall.

I watch her shadow follow her on the
wall opposite my office; the scent of
floral perfume and a million different
hair products lingers for a few seconds
until that, too, is gone.

A part of us is always tensing, I
realize, against things we love going
away.

FORTY

A little regret.

We celebrated our Happy Fifth Dating Anniversary on the coast.

While snuggled up on the King size bed with crisp white sheets, the ocean waves roaring outside the window, I presented Pete with a card.

And in the postscript, I said to please read this one blog post.

"Should I do it now?" Pete asked with a whiff of reluctance.

"Yes, now, please," I answered with more force than I intended.

That excessive force should have been a tip-off that the moment wasn't ripe for the conversation I had in mind. But I was too caught up in my agenda.

***

"Well?" I asked, finally, unable to contain my fidgets. "What do you think?"

"I think Nick Cave's writing is amazing, as always," Pete responded earnestly. The piece I had him read was relationship advice to a middle-aged woman who's in love with a man who's been divorced once and doesn't want to marry again.

"I know, but I'm asking you, what did you think of what Nick told the woman to tell her boyfriend?" I said, impatiently.

Pete pointed out that Nick Cave—yes, the musician—had given her so many points of view and options to consider; none were wrong. I nodded.

He also said that Nick advised the two to stay connected and intimate, even in their conflict, and move forward—not with an agenda, but with a daring heart. I nodded again.

"So, what are you asking me to give an opinion on?" Pete said, genuinely confused.

I thought about saying, *I want to know what you think of Nick thinking that the boyfriend changing his mind might be a wonderfully daring-hearted thing to do and if you think that's something you might consider for yourself?*

But I could see clearly now how convoluted my "Let's talk about getting married" plan had been.

I could see how scared I was to have a
daring heart, to open the
conversation, knowing Pete's
reservations about marriage.

So, I flashed the brightest, toothiest
smile I could and said, "Nothing."

FORTY-ONE

Vienna waits for you.

I remember when I first played a tune for Reina from the A-side of *The Stranger*. The song was *Just the Way You Are*. She was eight years old then, and we were driving with a friend to the Lynnwood swimming pool for splash time at the water park.

Reina leaned forward in the back seat, and asked me, "What's a song that's like a soundtrack to your childhood when you were my age?"

She giggled at my answer.

"Mom, did you say, *Just the Way You Are*?" she said, barely containing her eyeroll. "I'm sorry, but I'm pretty sure Bruno Mars wasn't born yet when you were little."

I didn't play Vienna for her that day or even later. I never expected her to like my old people's music.

And even though I continued to lament that missed opportunity to see Billy Joel at "The Garden" back in the nineties, I didn't think she cared or noticed.

But suddenly, in the spring of 2023, it became clear she'd found the best song on the B-side herself. I heard it playing in her room virtually every morning, and sometimes also in the evenings. From my office, I heard Billy Joel crooning to her:

"Slow down, you're doing fine . . . you can't be everything you want be before your time. . ."

Vienna was the soundtrack to Reina's
fifteen-year-old life.

****

Fast forward to July, one day after
Reina turned sixteen.

Pete squeezed my hand as we sat in a
darkened room and watched tears
stream down Reina's face as the Piano
Man played her favorite song from my
favorite album—live in New York City.
At "The Garden."

Sometimes, plans go awry. And one
plan gone awry incites a chain
reaction, leading to an unending mess
of broken plans and promises.

You think you already know what's on
the horizon, that you can predict
what's at the end of the road, so you
carry on with a stiff upper lip stiff and
a guarded, shattered heart.

Then one day, you're going about your
Plan B or C or Z, and you look up at the
garden that's sprung up.

To your astonishment, it is lovely—
and alive, fragrant, impossibly
generative, and generous from the
roots to the tips. The beauty is
immersive. It takes your breath away.

I looked around "The Garden" in awe
of all the moments that led to this one.

I squeezed Pete's hand back, tears
streaming down my cheeks, just like
Reina's.

And Billy Joel was right; Vienna waited
for me, just like he said it would.

FORTY-TWO

Alive.

It's true what Pete said back in 2016: well-tended Japanese gardens are narratives.

Their grasses, camellias, azaleas, and maples bloom, wilt, sprout, and bloom again.

Our garden gets threatened with pests and diseases, welcome wild friends, bury those same friends, bend with the wind, sing with the birds, receive the seeds they carry, thirst one day and dissolve into a muddy puddle on another. The rocks chip and tumble, the boulders grow a soft covering of moss.

Rain or shine, in winter, spring,
summer, or fall, gardens are forever
transitional and transitioning;
transformative and transforming.

We can't say for sure what will live
and what will die.

We can't guarantee it'll look the way
we want it to in the distant future.

But we can be sure it'll be achingly,
frustratingly beautiful.

That's just what I want for us: an
achingly, frustratingly beautiful
garden of a life together forever.

So, I decide to try, try again, for reals
this time, to reach across the divide to
seek out his hands, to say what's on
my heart.

I decide I will tell Pete that it'd be
great for us to get married.

FORTY-THREE

The soft animal of our bodies.

It's now April 2024. I'm driving, he's riding shotgun. It's drizzling lightly enough to be pretty; I don't need to turn on the windshield wipers.

To the right, I see workboats with aluminum hulls floating in steely but calm waters. Spent cherry blossoms are everywhere, thickly covering the sidewalks with pale pink confetti.

The sky is gray but not heavy. The days are rapidly getting longer.

It's a Monday, and we're talking about the logistics of the week ahead.

"Do you have time to pick up the
wedding band I ordered?" I ask.
I get the answer from a warm hand
over my right knee; it's saying yes
with a light, long squeeze.

"I'm looking forward to being married
to you," Pete says.

I place my hand on the hand resting
on my knee.

 "Me, too," I say with a smile, and
squeeze back.

***

So here we are, at the end, which is
also the beginning.

We are moving forward, moment by
moment, and letting the soft animal of

our often-lonely bodies love what they
love.

Meanwhile, because it's April in the
Pacific Northwest, the wild geese are
somewhere in the high sky, heading
home again, telling each other of their
despair.

Their echoes and circular movements
remind us that the world goes on.

And they call to us, harsh and
exciting—

Over and over, announcing our place,
right here in the family of things.

I made a playlist for you.

Enjoy music that perfectly accompanies this book + journaling prompts, book club resources, and bonus essays at **iwanthisforus.com**

Acknowledgments.

Rhythm and togetherness are the backbone of creative work.

I wrote 90% of this book on Monday co-drafting sessions at Story Republic, one forty-minute session at a time. Thank you for holding me lovingly accountable: Andrea, Anne, April, Bernadette, Caroline, Carolyn, Cat, Dave, Enrika, Gary, Jackie, Jacquie, Jeff, John, Leanne, Mandell, Michael, Michelle, Sabah, Shannon, Susan, and Terry.

Some of my workshopping happens at the Wednesday Workout Live Storytelling Sessions hosted by the incomparable Michael Averill; and

Michelle Spencer, with her wit and steadfast company, bolsters my confidence on Humpday afternoons.

On Thursdays, I post a fresh *Nudge* on Substack. Bryony, Cat, David, Donald, Joanna, Julie, Lacey, Lisa, Lyle, Marian, Mary Anne, Michelle, Pam, Peg, Roberta, Teri Jo, and Stephanie, you are especially great at cheering me on. Your love means everything. Thank you.

I wouldn't be here without my my bi-monthly Sunday Brave Writers Group meetings—thank you Elle and Simone for being my heart of hearts.

And I never would've become a writer without my Monday Mastermind Meetings (going strong for twelve years and counting; thanks Jen, Terrace, and Ursula!)

This is my third book, and I decided I wouldn't do any part of book creation alone. Dave, Hana, Renee, Sabah, and Simone for said yes to joining the fledgling *Your Tiny Beautiful Book* community and made books with me. Look what we made happen!

Behind the scenes, Beth Pagano fills my phone with memes—and thought-provoking Brianna Wiest quotes—every single freaking day at 3 p.m. Emojis are her love language, and they quite literally keep me alive.

Thank you, Kai and Reina. Wanting you to be as proud of me as I am keeps me on my toes and makes me braver than I think I can.

And all my love, of course, to Pete. I can't believe you trusted me carte blanche to write this book. Coffee is your other language, and I aspire to reciprocate.

Finally, thank *you*, yes you dear
reader, for sticking with me all the
way through to this page.

Whatever your story and whatever
your dream, please bring it forward,
they have a place in my heart already.

OTHER TITLES BY THE AUTHOR

*I Want To Remember This:
Recognizing the Tiny
Moments That Make Up a Life*

*I Want This For You:
Mothering What Matters Most*

*What is Love? A Story
Collection (editor)*

The Garden Meditations Deck

ABOUT THE AUTHOR

Rumi Tsuchihashi is a champion of tiny, beautiful things and their power to radically change lives. Her first book, *I Want To Remember This: Recognizing the Tiny Moments That Make Up a Life*, led to the publication of a 100-word in the *New York Times*. To learn about her books and programs, go to HelloRumi.co.

www.ingramcontent.com/pod-product-compliance
Lightning Source LLC
Chambersburg PA
CBHW062219150726
47991CB00006B/2343